# Ping the spider™

## Phonics 3

Pre     K     1st     2nd

Cub

Gum

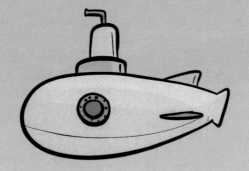

Sub

Tub

Cup

Pup

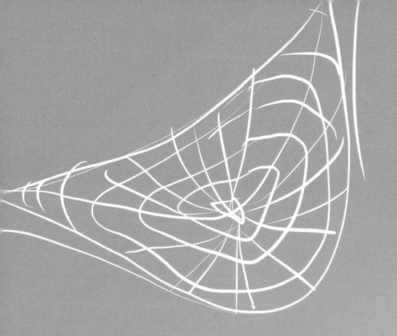

Web

Up

Gas

Yam

Mom

Hop

Mud

Bus

Ant

Elf

Elk

Bee

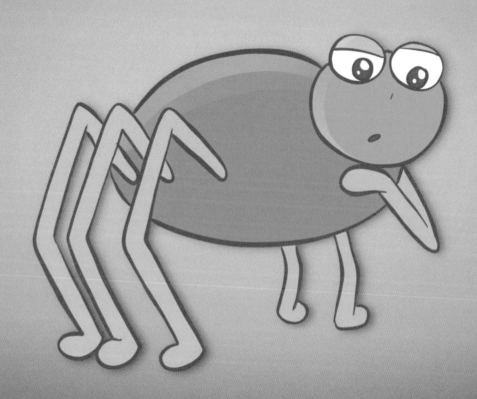

This book is a little harder than the first two.
The rest of the pages won't have pictures with them.
Good luck!

Bud

Us

Zip

Him

Yes

Sum

Sup

Hem

End

Odd

Rub

Hum

Inn

Off

Tim

Pam

Mel

Bob

Jan

Ann

Kim

Ned

Sam

Tom

Ben

Jim

Meg

Ted

An

Am

Ken

Dan

As

At

Wasn't that fun?
Let's try that again,
learning phonics,
with Ping and his friends!